Little Square Coloring Book™

Kaleidoscopes to Color For Kids

Michael F. Parsons

Published by
T. A. Francis Publishing
tafpub.com

First Edition
October, 2015

ISBN:978-1-944065-08-9

I realize that this book is actually a rectangle.
Squares are a special type of rectangle so I suppose this series should be called 'Little Rectangular Coloring Book'.

But that's silly.

Feel free to color these kaleidoscopes as portraits, landscapes or anything you like!

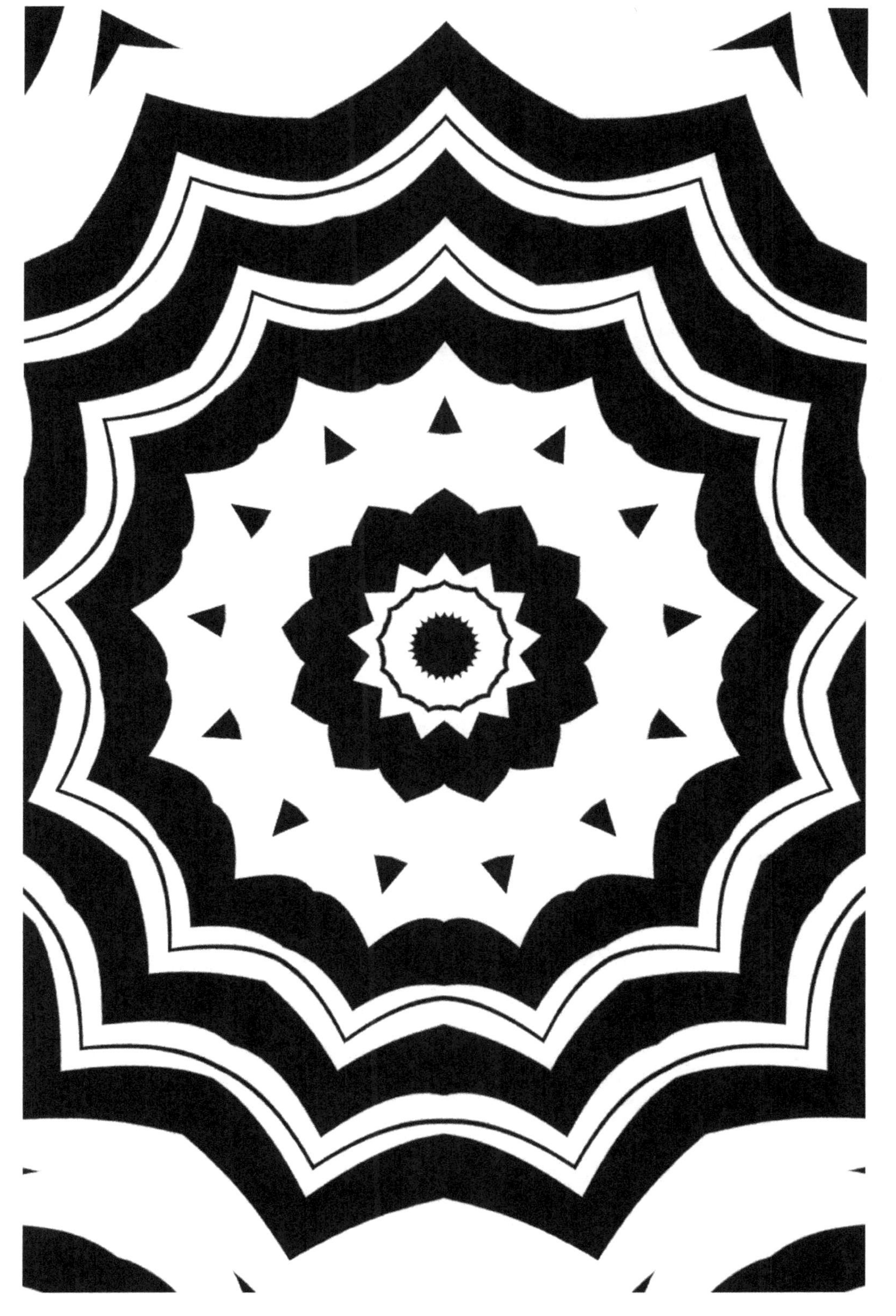

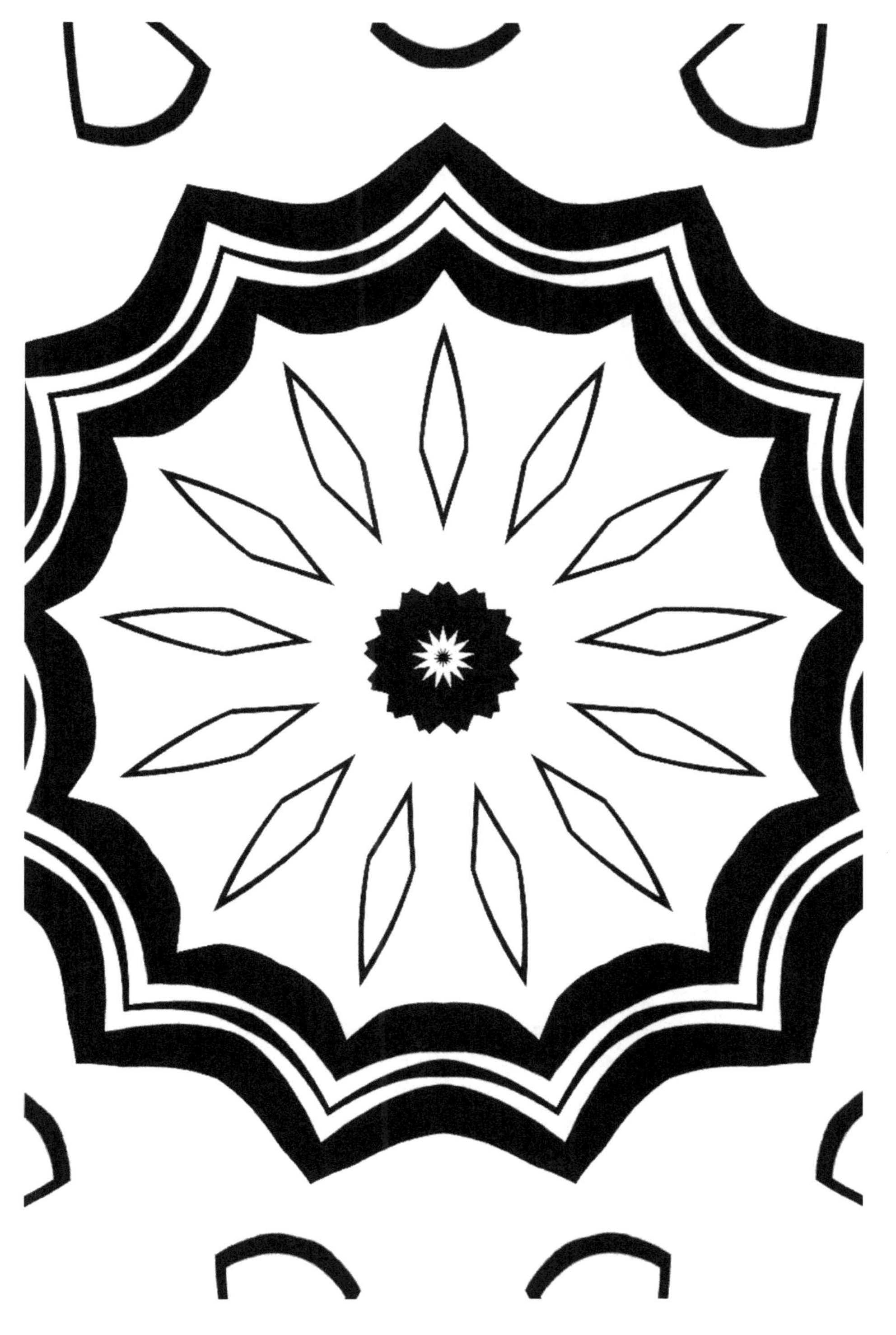

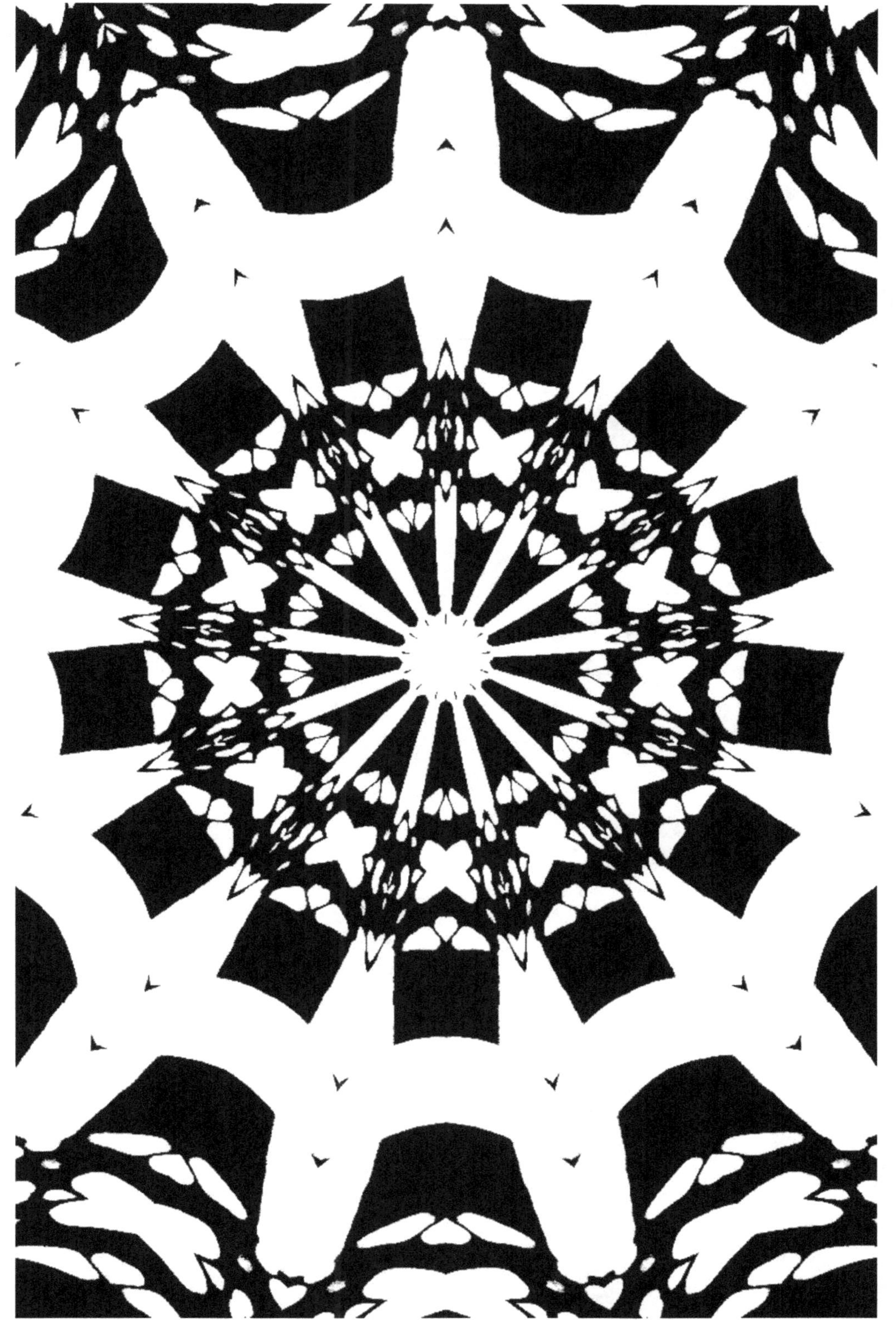

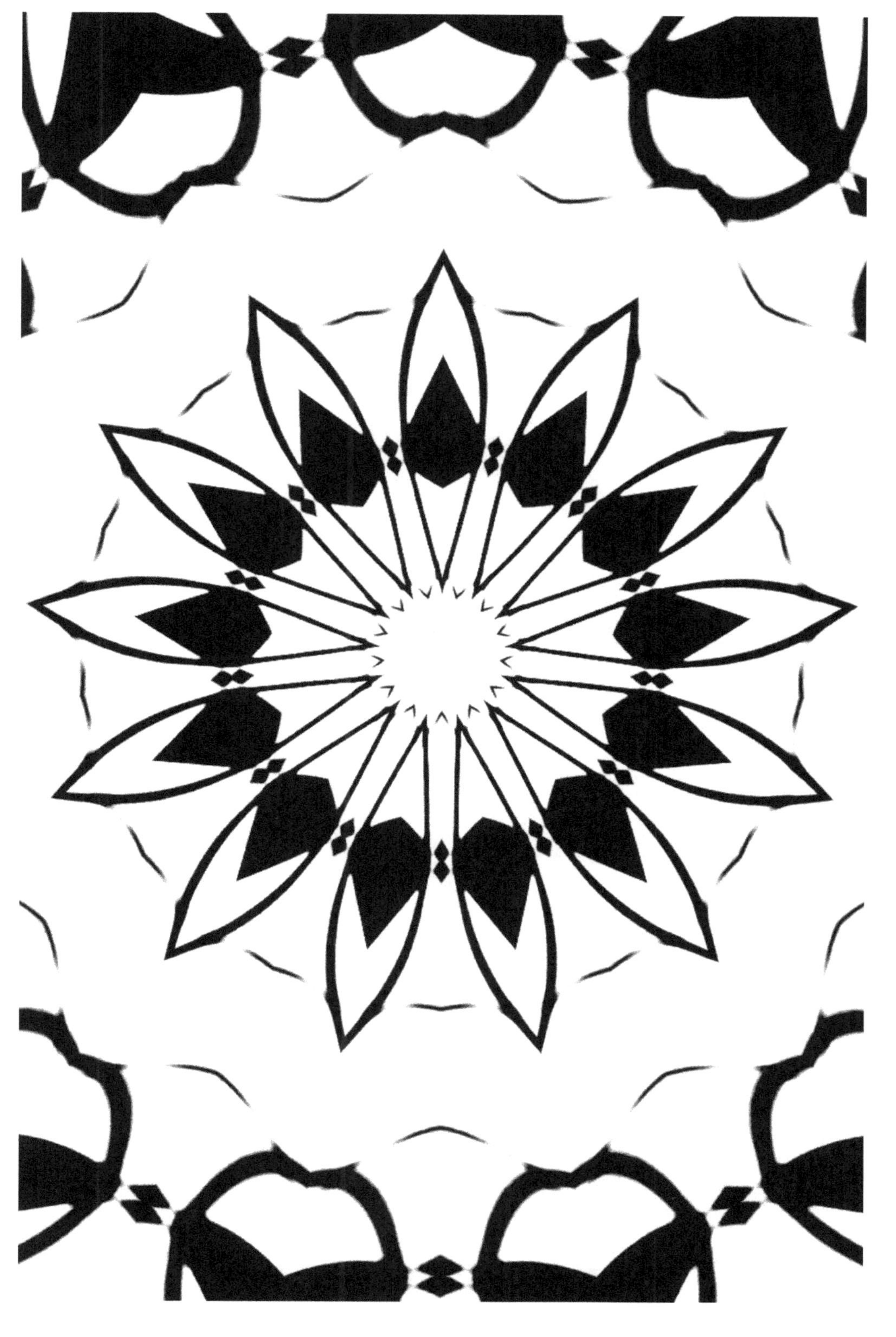

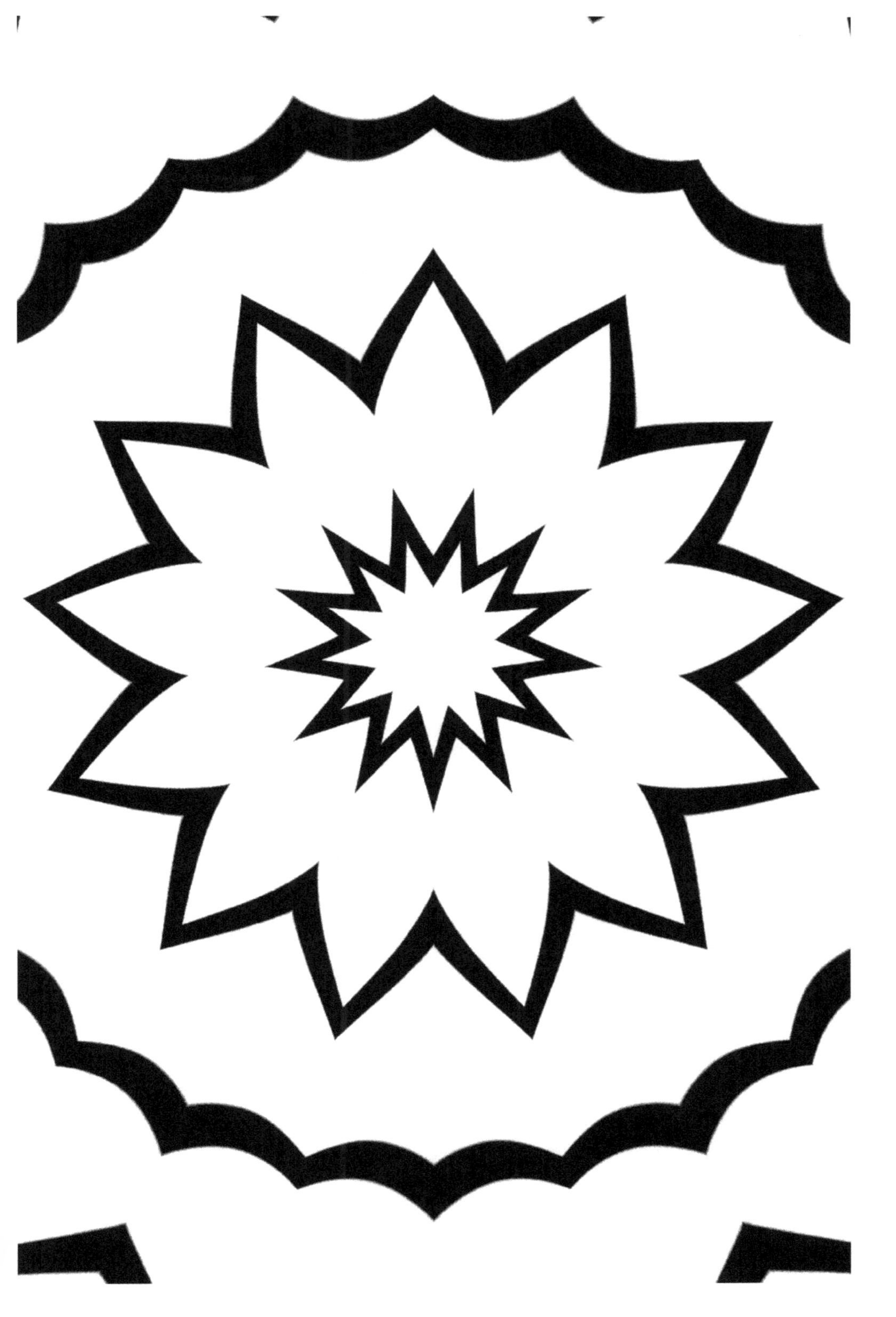

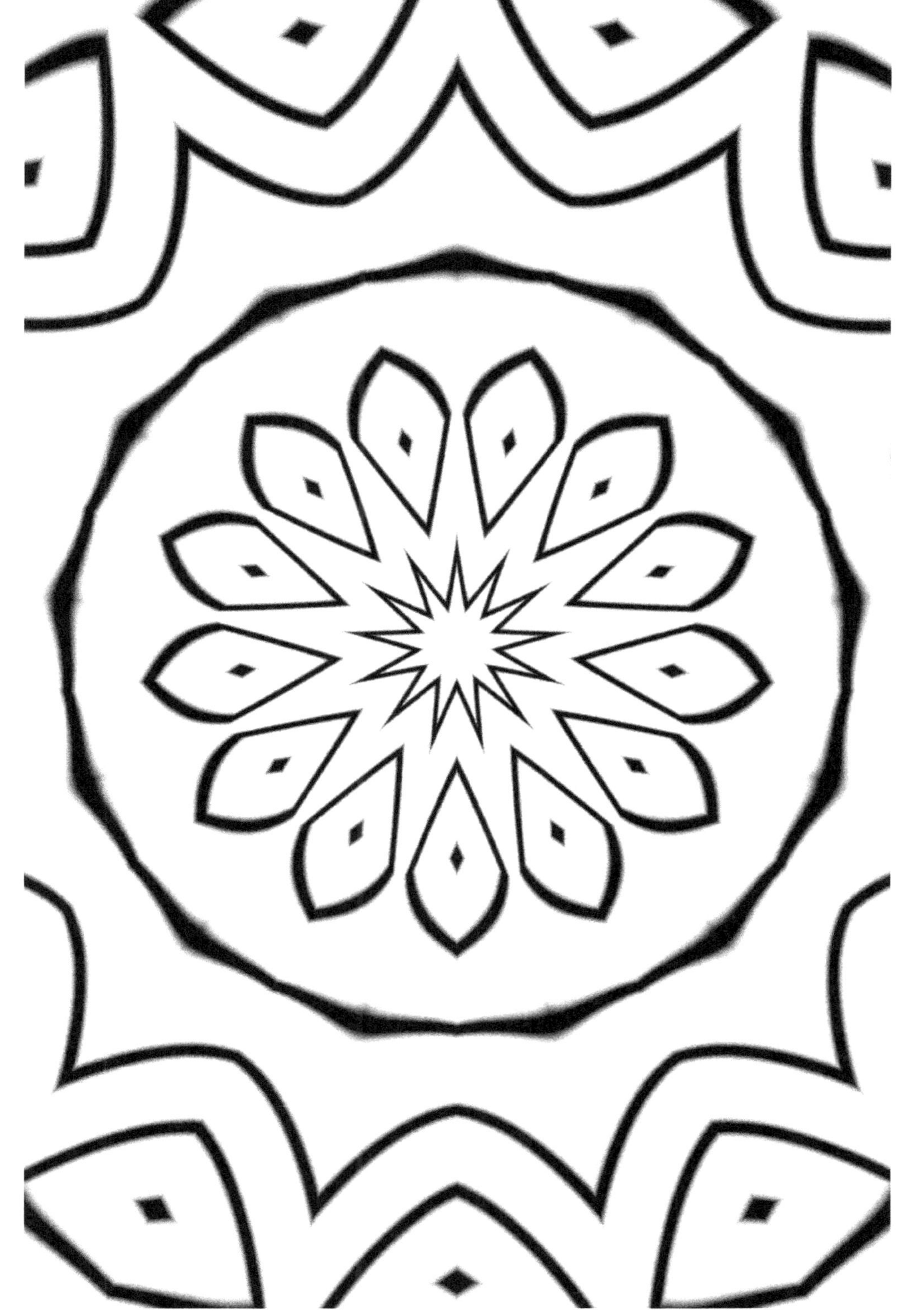

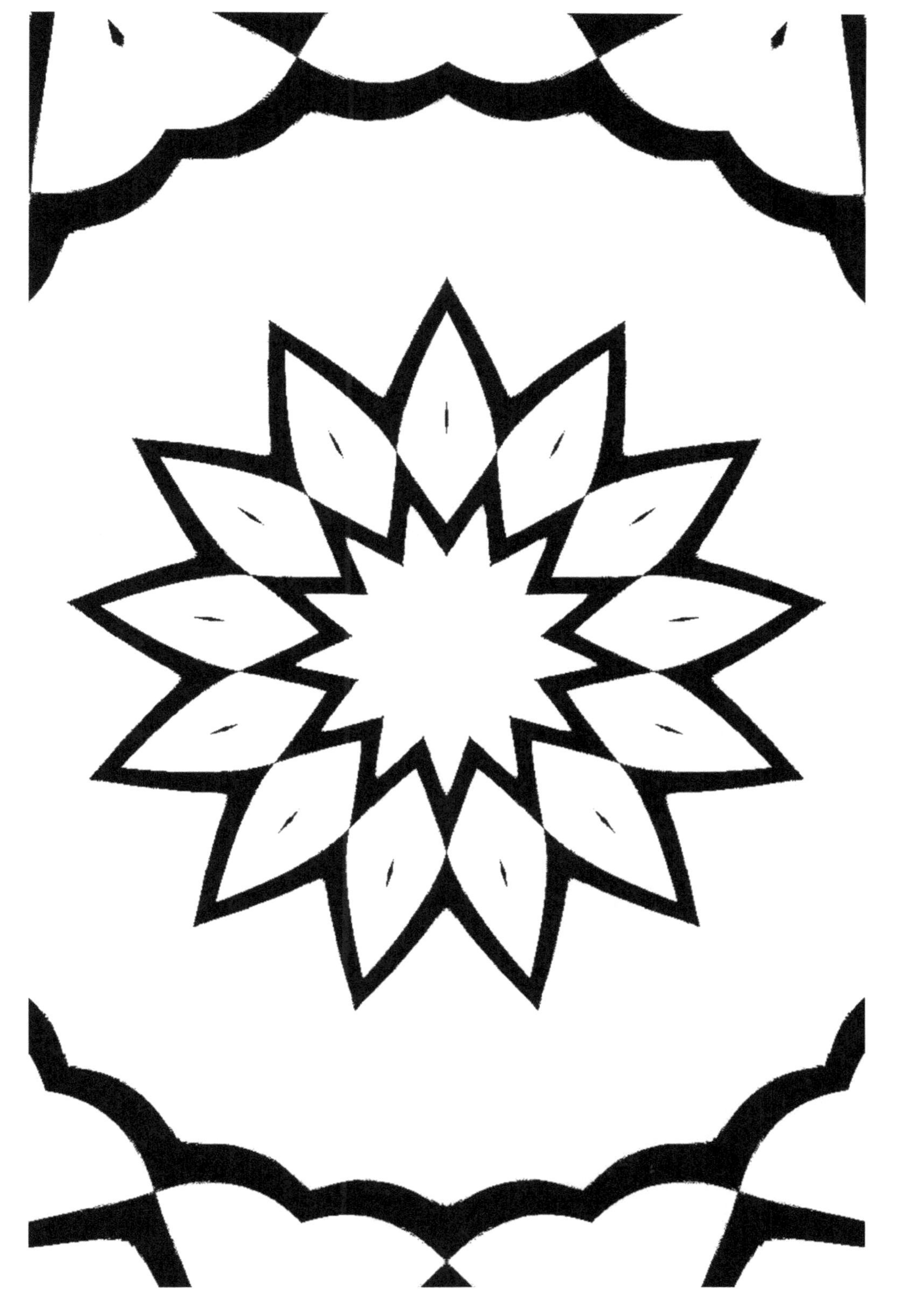

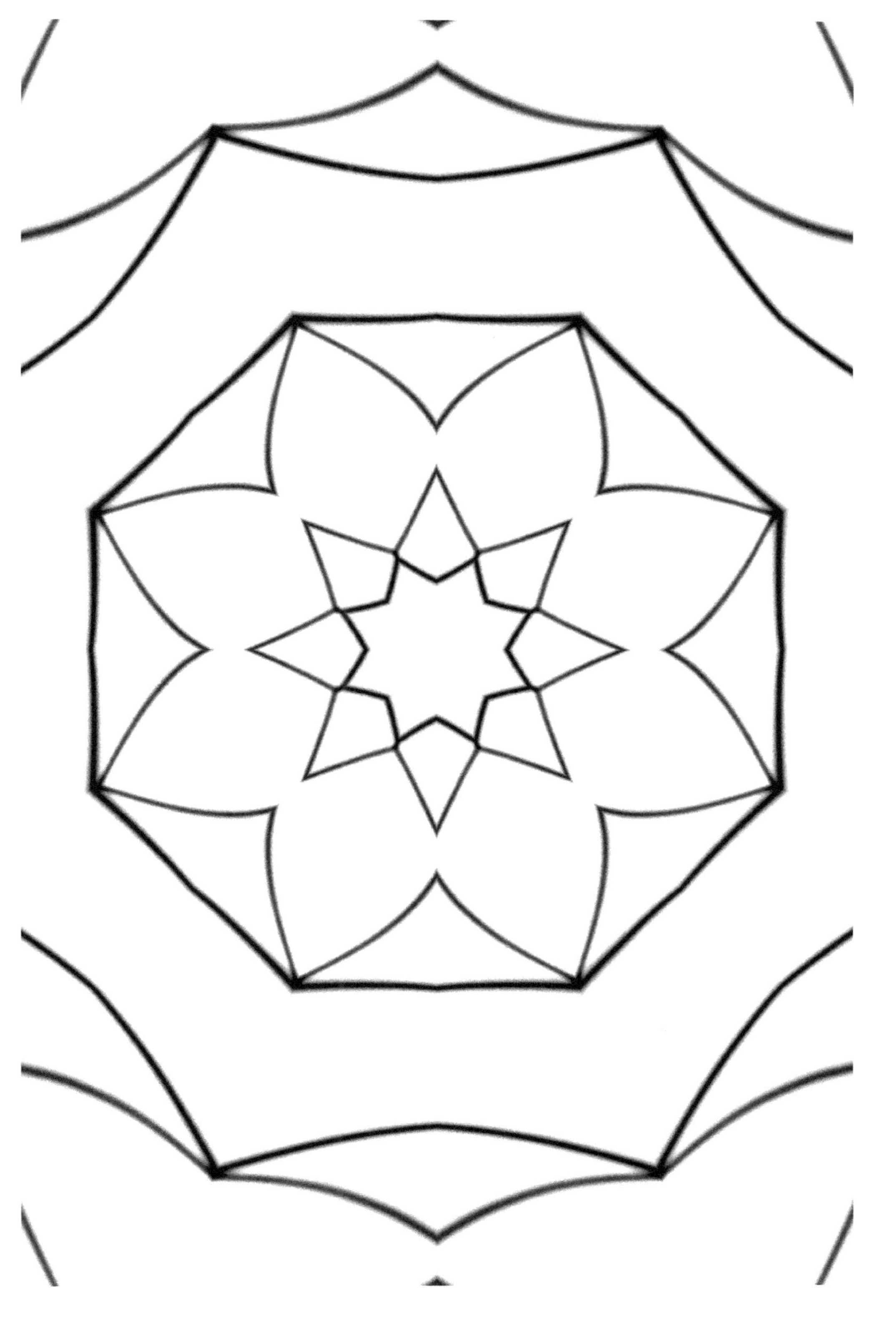

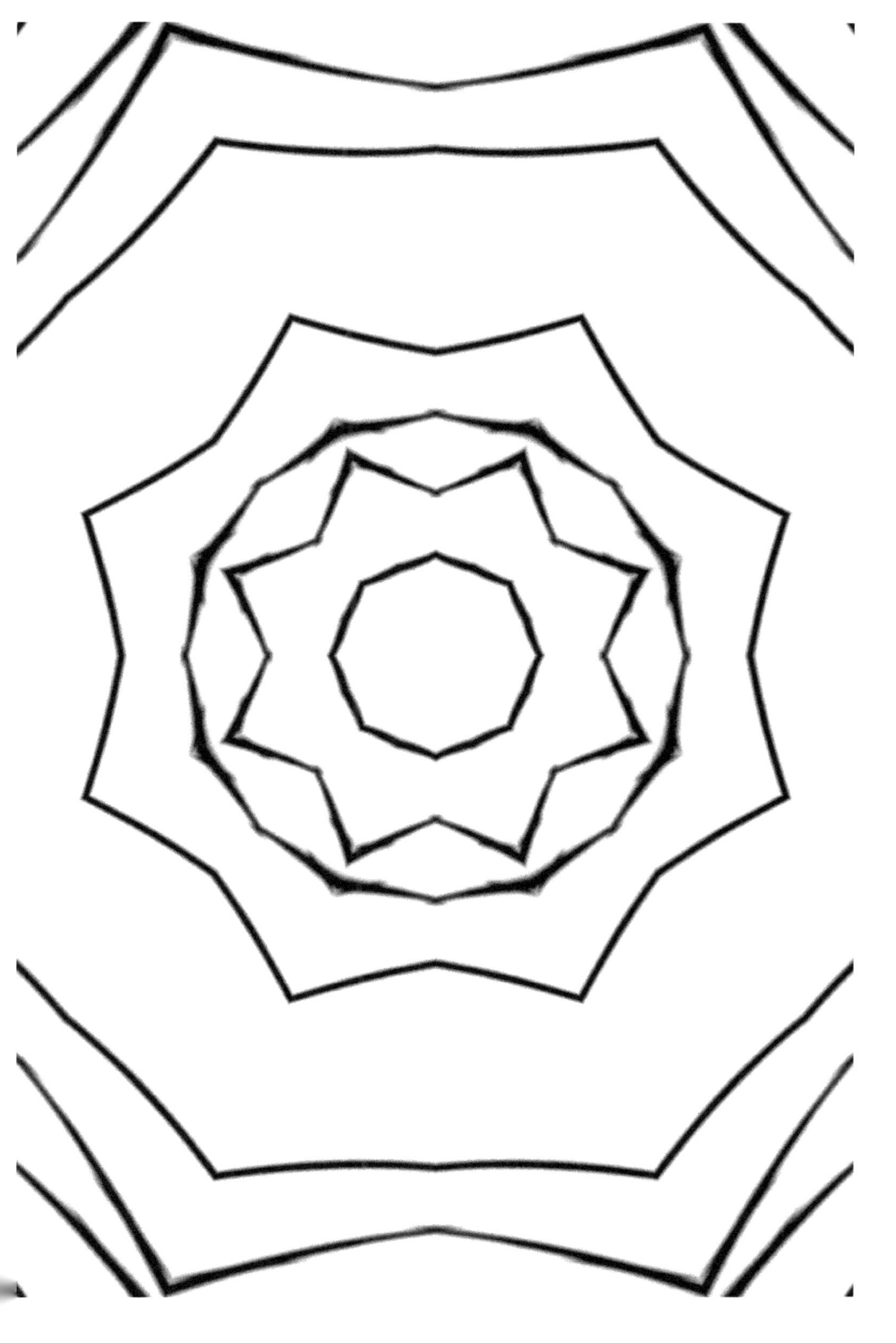

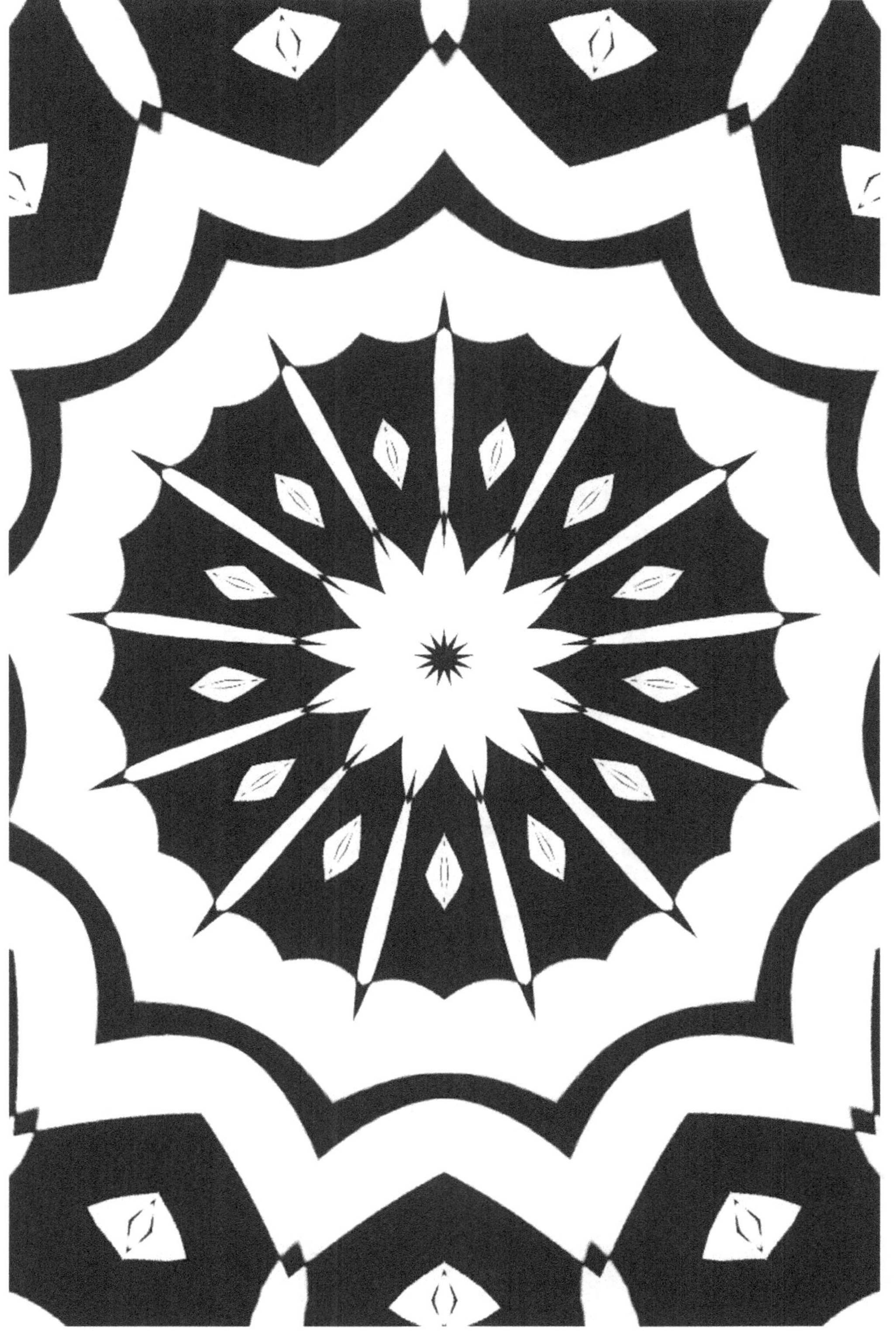

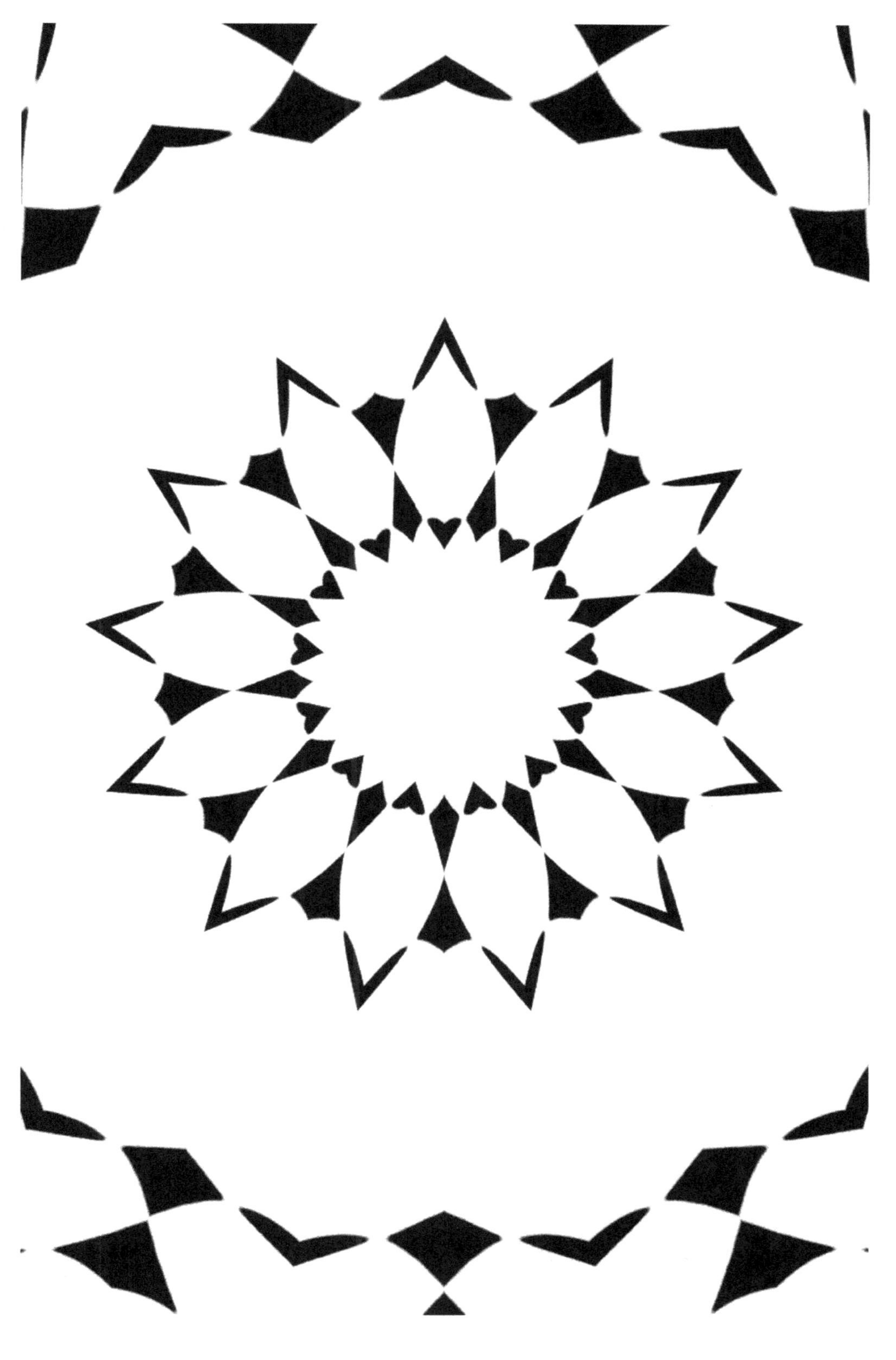

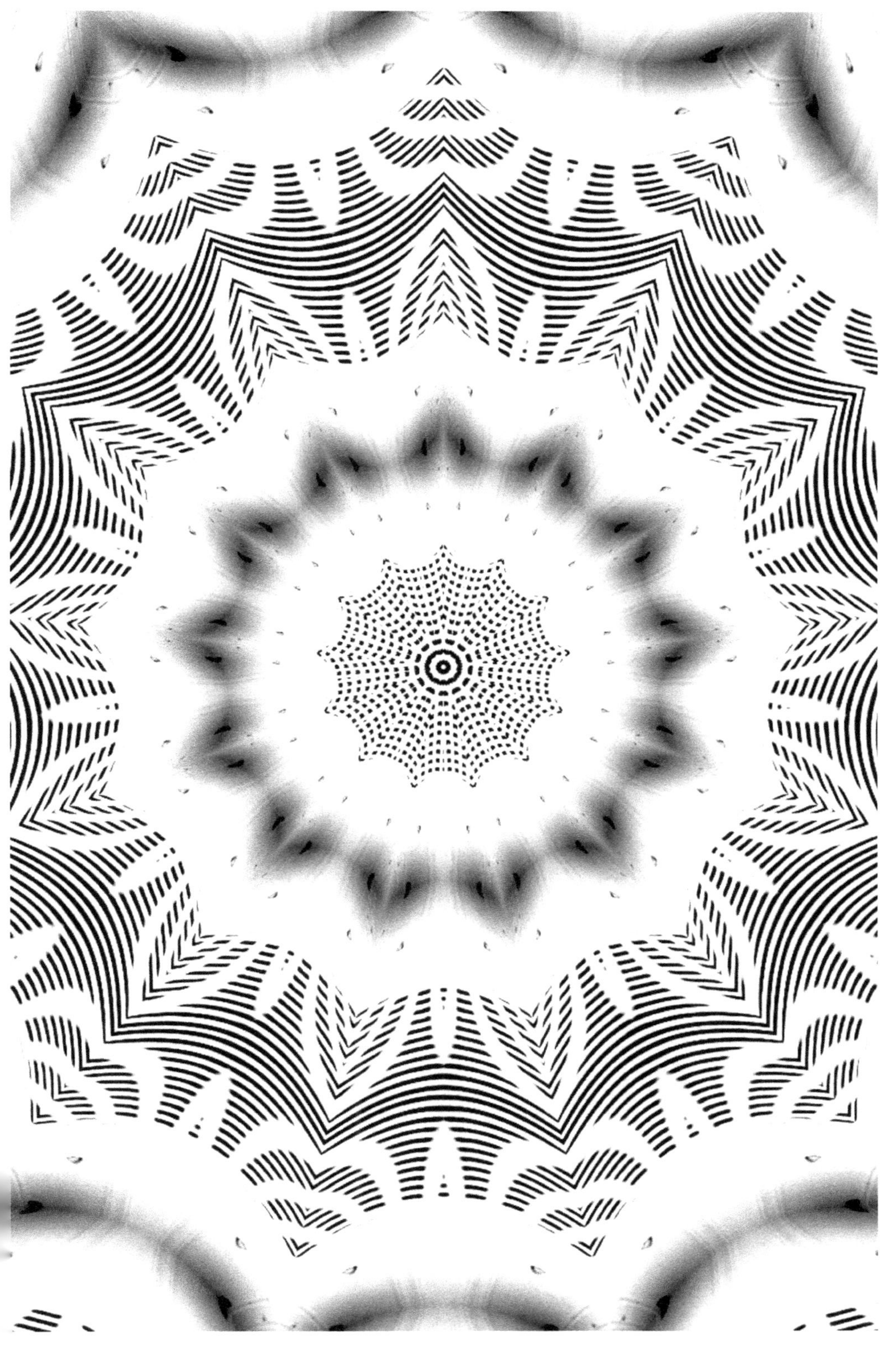

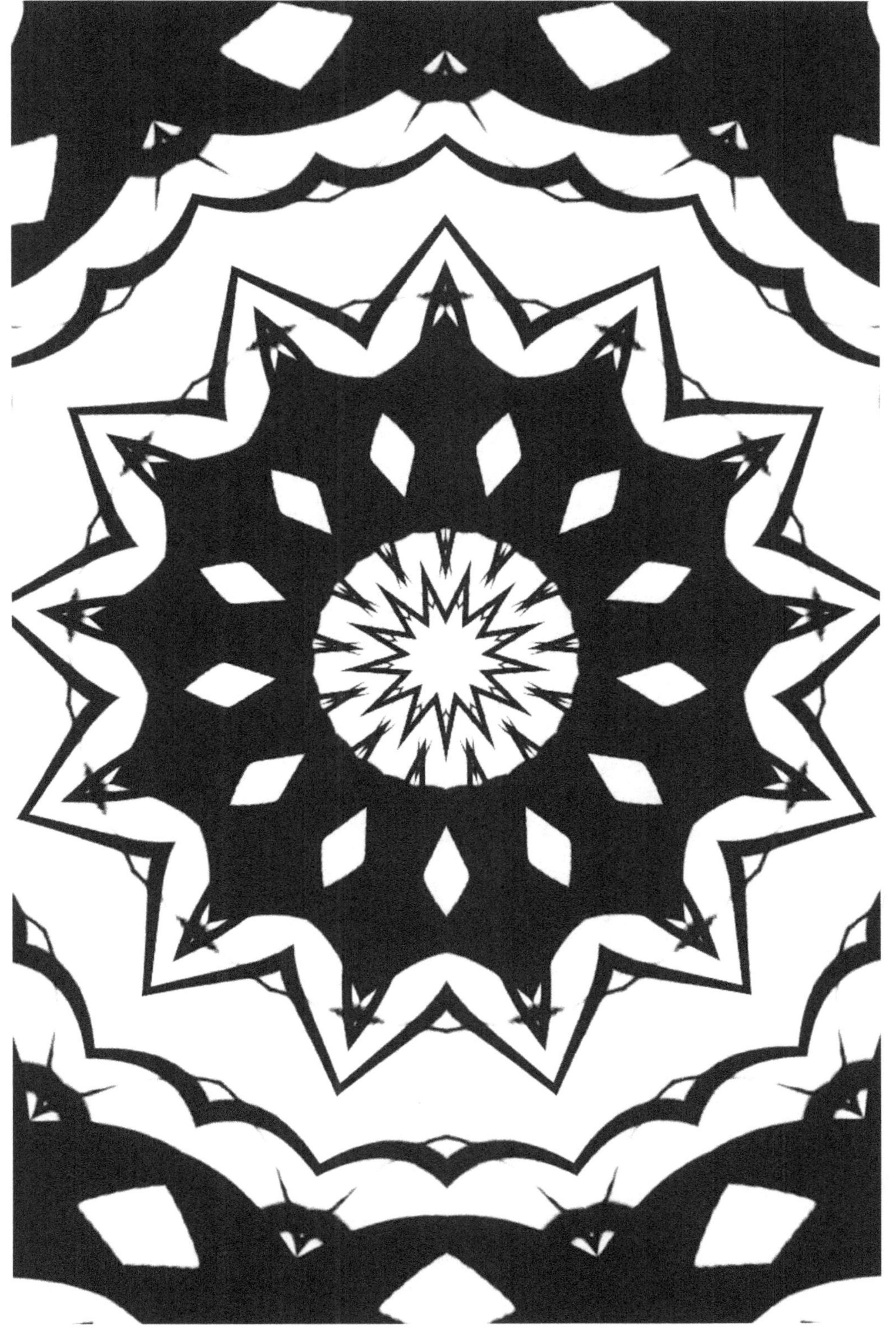

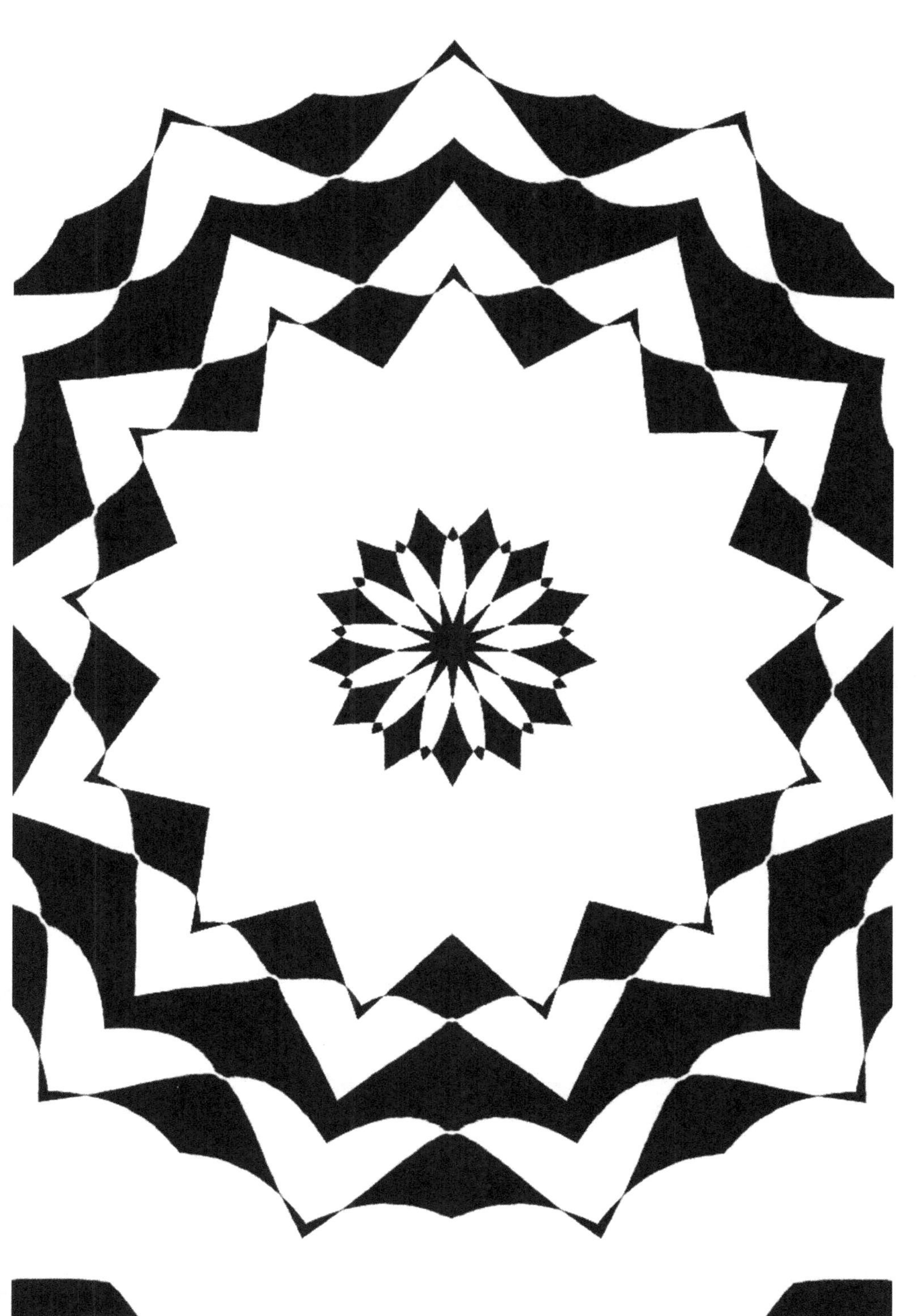

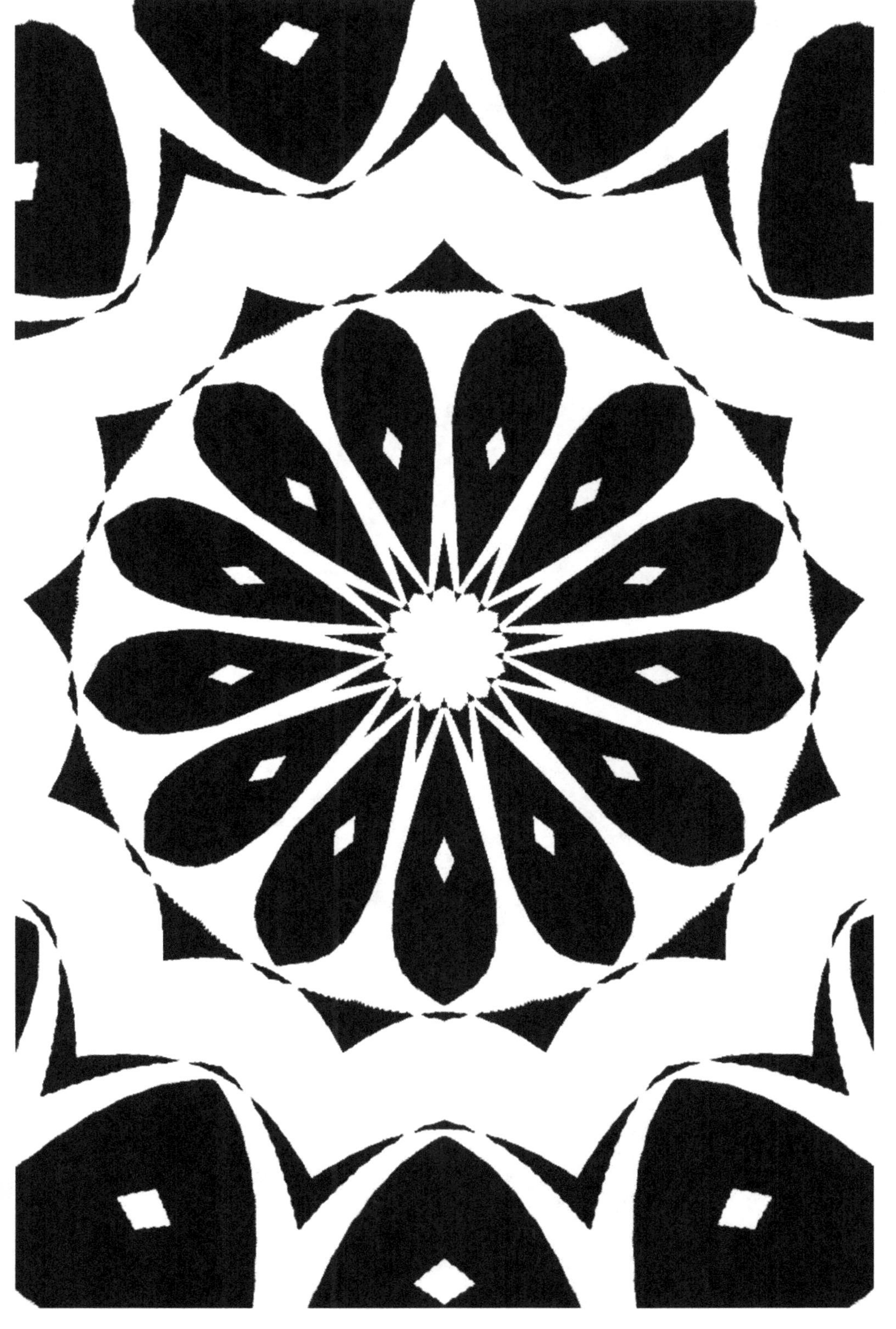

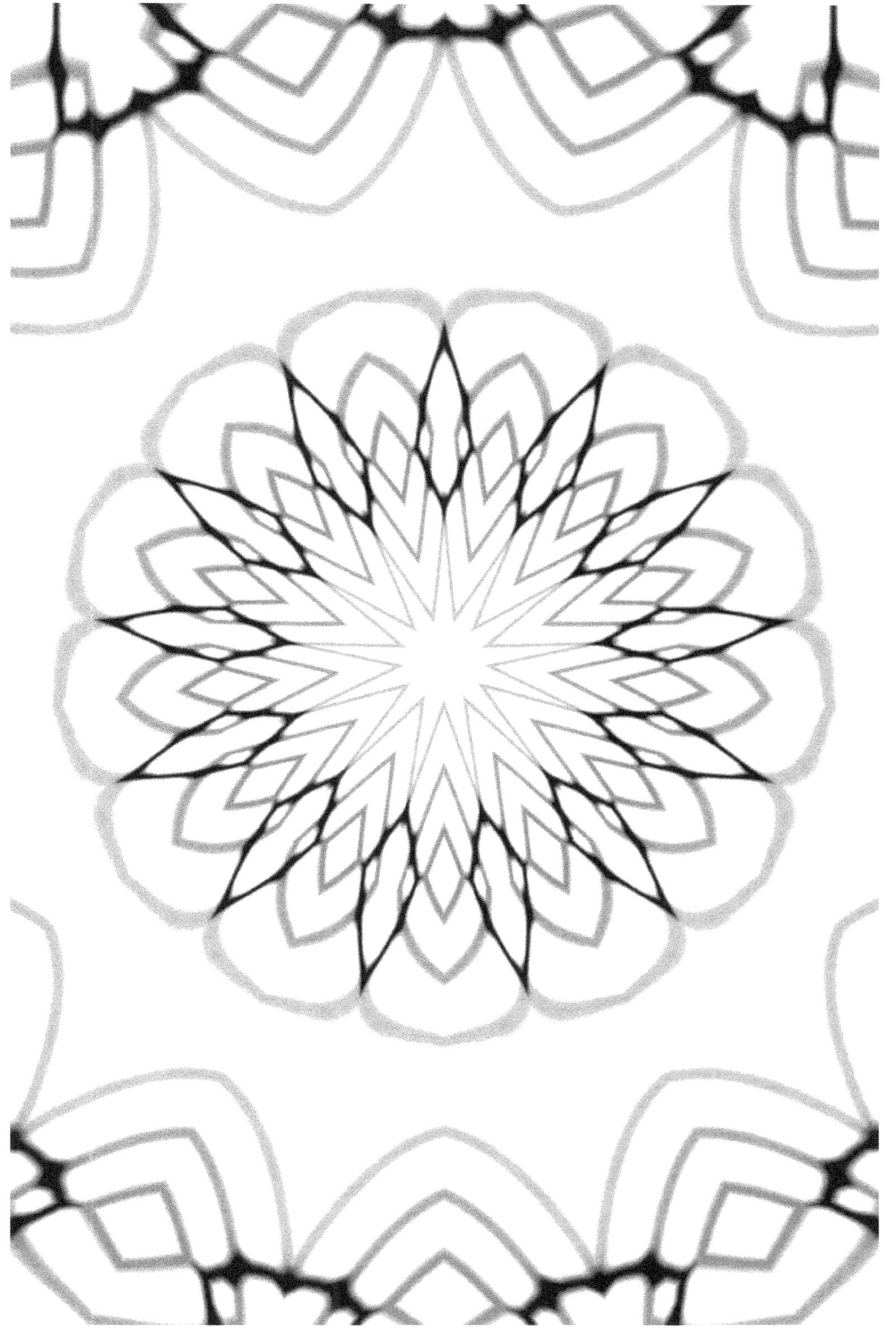

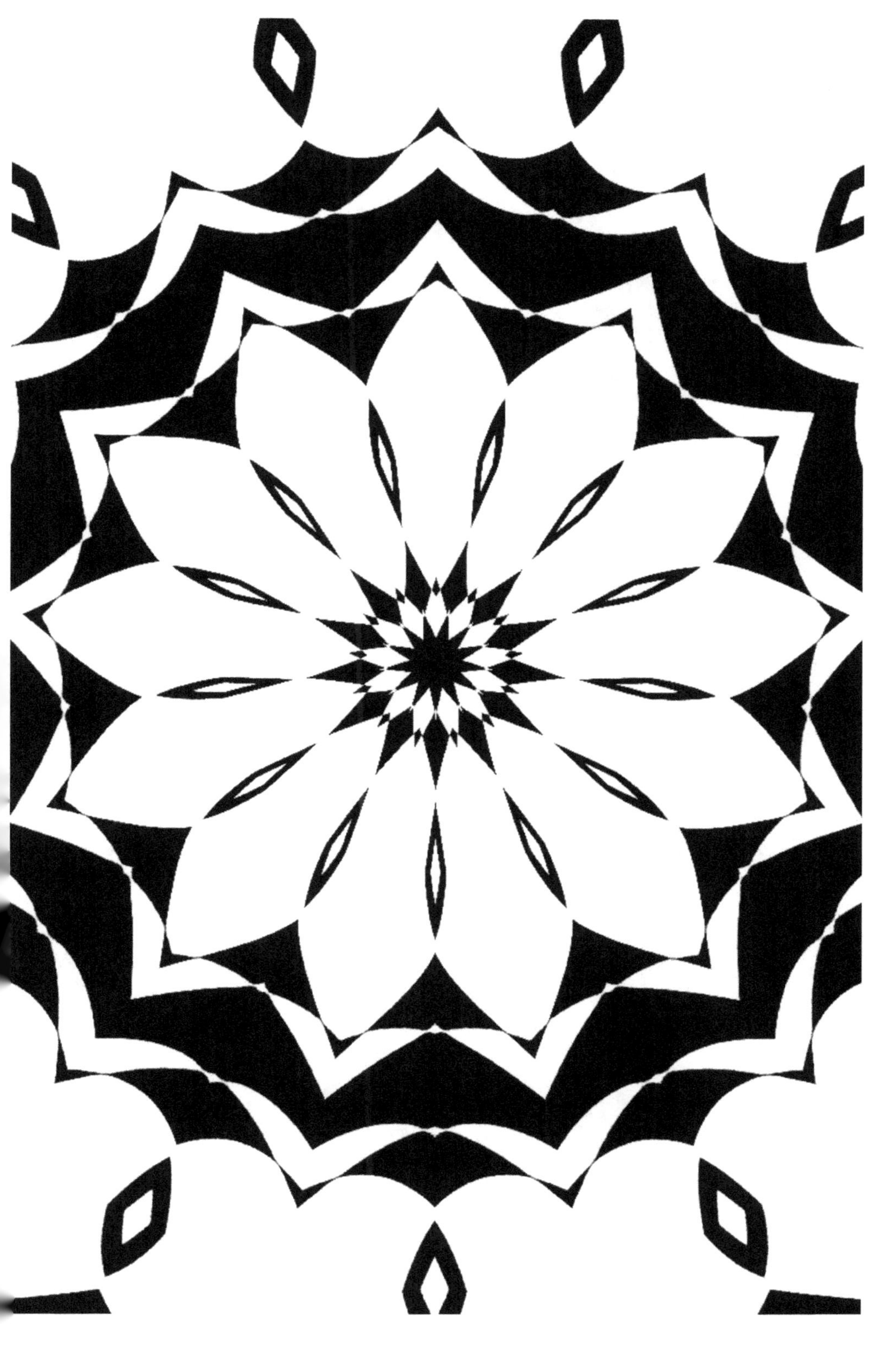

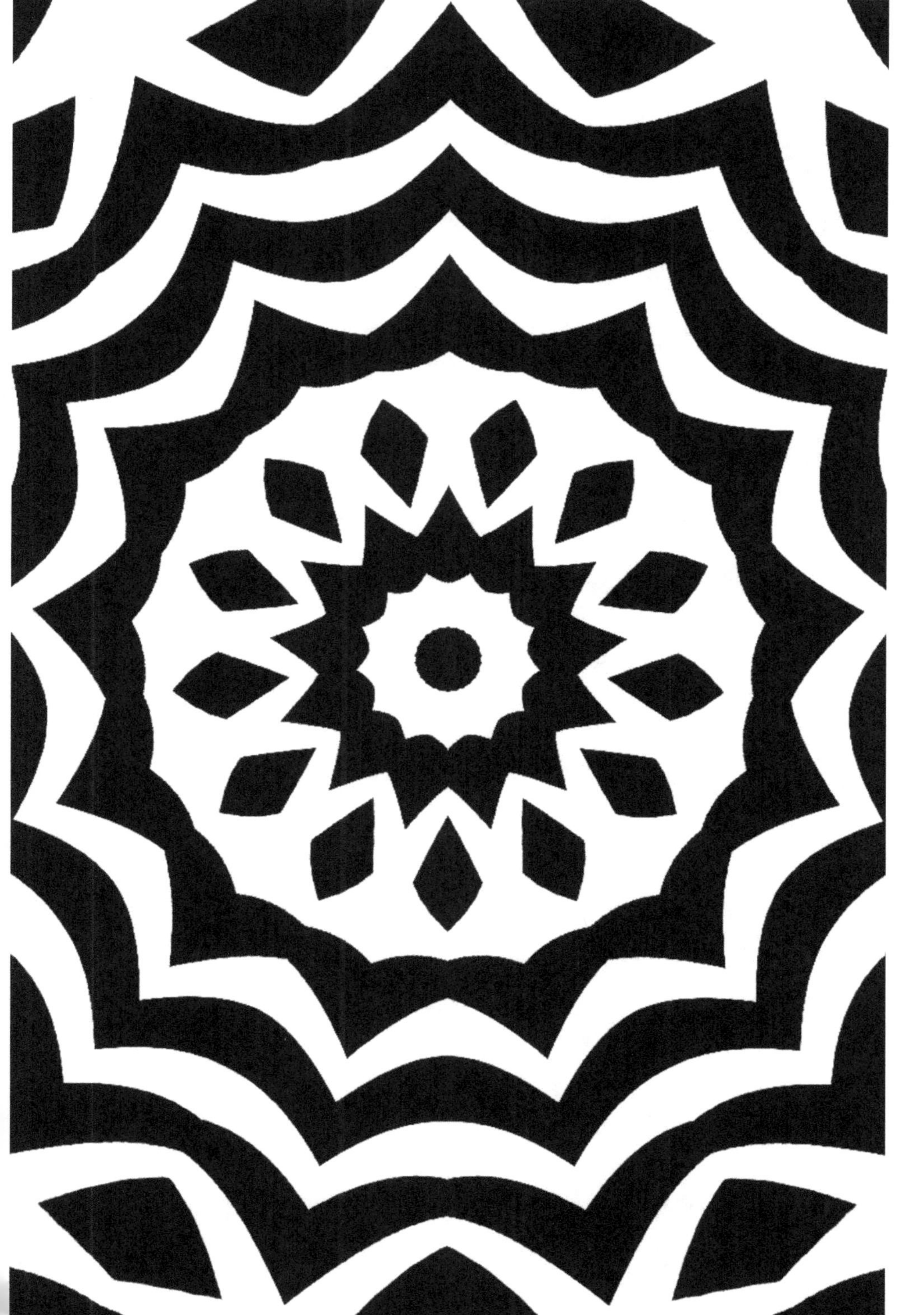

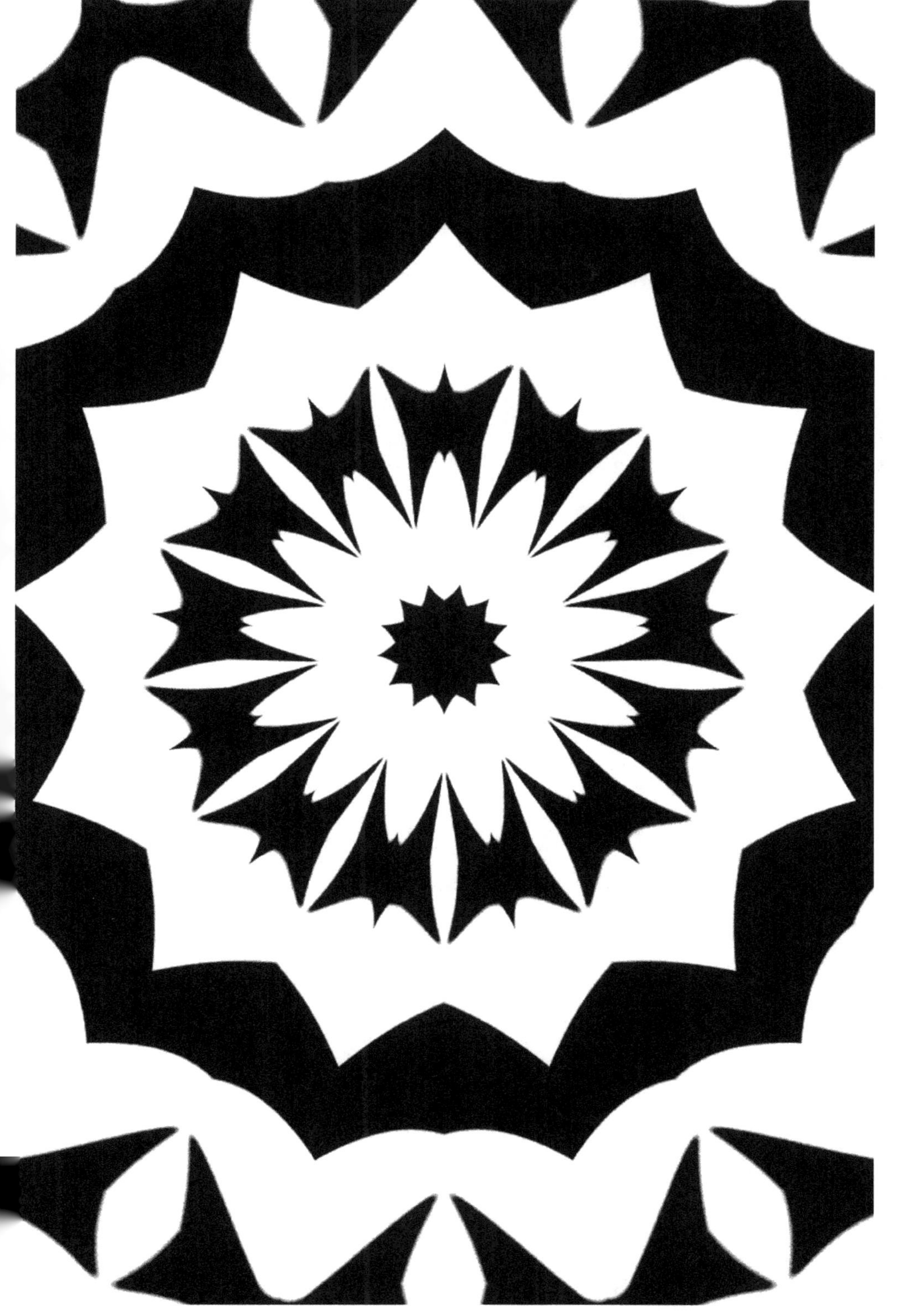

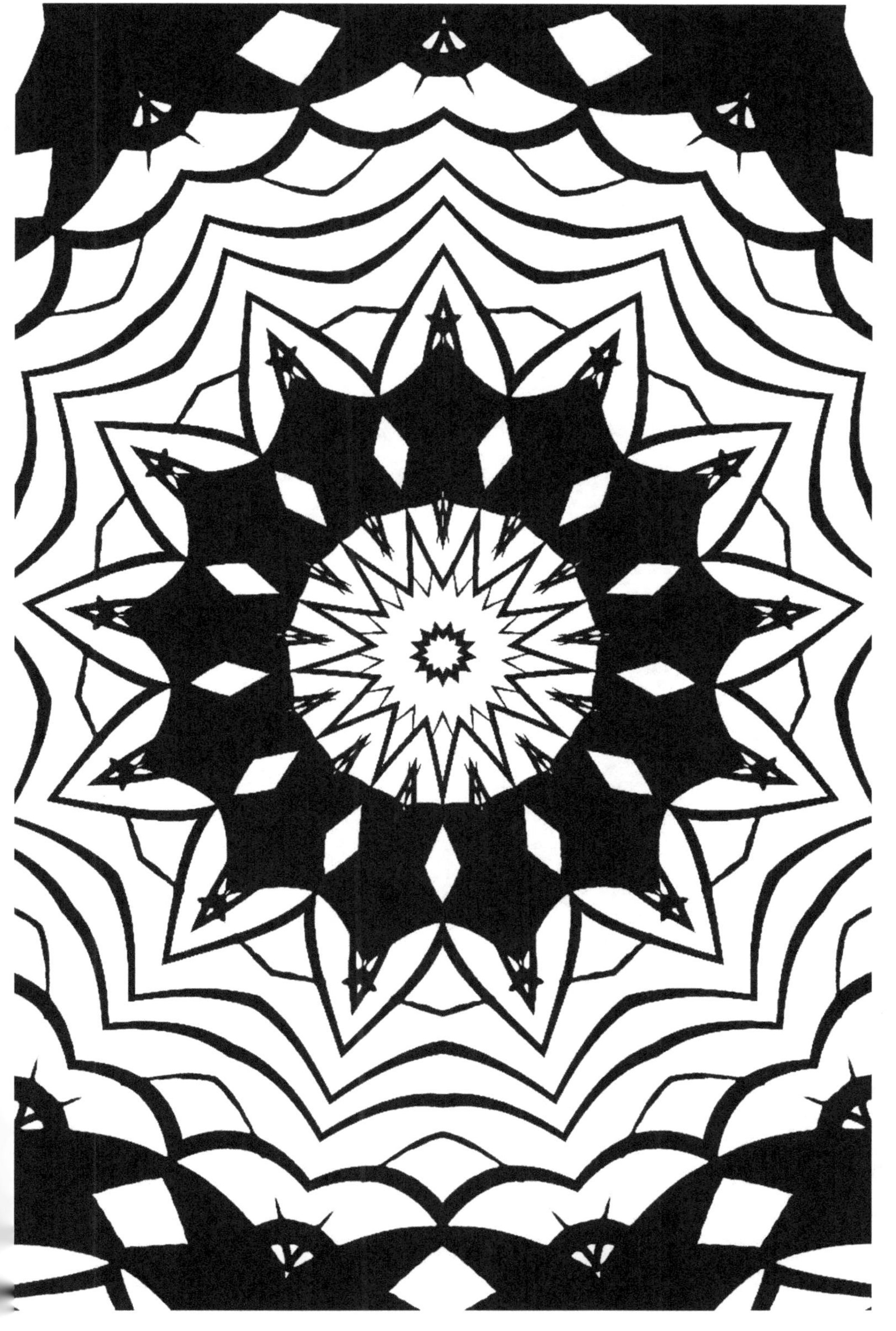

Thank you for spending some of your time with our "Little Square Coloring Book: Kaleidoscopes to Color for Kids". I hope you enjoyed it.

If you'd like to join our "Artist's Group" to keep up to date on new coloring books and get a free, printable PDF 'Sampler Book' via email (which is different from this book), please visit

http://LittleSquareColoringBook.com/Artists-Group

or use your mobile device to scan the QR code below.

Little Square Coloring Book

Current and Future Releases

Samplers

September and October 2015 Sampler

ISBN: 978-1-944065-10-2

November and December 2015 Sampler

ISBN: 978-1-944065-15-7

Geometric Mandalas

For Kids#1 ISBN: 978-1-944065-00-3

For Kids #2 ISBN: 978-1-944065-12-6

For Kids #3 ISBN: 978-1-944065-13-3

For Young Artists and Older Eyes#1

ISBN: 978-1-944065-01-0

For Young Artists and Older Eyes #2

ISBN: 978-1-944065-16-4

For Adults#1 ISBN: 978-1-944065-04-1

For Adults #2 ISBN: 978-1-944065-11-9

Challenger Edition #1 ISBN: 978-1-944065-03-4

Challenger Edition #1 ISBN: 978-1-944065-14-0

Spheres and Abstracts
Book One ISBN: 978-1-944065-05-8
Book Two ISBN: 978-1-944065-17-1

Groovy Geometrics
For Kids ISBN: 978-1-944065-06-5
For Kids #2 ISBN: 978-1-944065-19-5
For Kids#3 ISBN: 978-1-944065-20-1
For Adults ISBN: 978-1-944065-02-7
For Adults#2 ISBN: 978-1-944065-21-8
Challenger Edition#1 ISBN: 978-1-944065-07-2
Challenger Edition #2 ISBN: 978-1-944065-18-8

Kaleidoscopes to Color
For Kids ISBN: 978-1-944065-08-9
For Kids#2 ISBN: 978-1-944065-22-5
For Kids #3 ISBN: 978-1-944065-23-2
For Adults ISBN: 978-1-944065-09-6
For Adults #2 ISBN: 978-1-944065-24-9
Challenger Edition ISBN: 978-1-944065-25-6

Complete Collections

Mandala Complete Collection
For Kids ISBN: 978-1-944065-26-3
For Young Adults and Older Eyes ISBN: 978-1-944065-99-7
For Adults ISBN: 978-1-944065-44-7
Challenger Edition ISBN: 978-1-944065-50-8

Spheres and Abstracts Complete Collection
ISBN: 978-1-944065-27-0

Groovy Geometrics Complete Collection
For Kids ISBN: 978-1-944065-67-6
For Adults ISBN: 978-1-944065-93-5
Challenger Edition ISBN: 978-1-944065-51-5

Kaleidoscopes to Color Complete Collection
For Kids ISBN: 978-1-944065-69-0

For Adults ISBN: 978-1-944065-38-6
Challenger Edition ISBN: 978-1-944065-53-9

Combo Packs

<u>Mandalas & Geometrics</u>

For Kids #1 ISBN: 978-1-944065-32-4
For Kids #2 ISBN: 978-1-944065-48-5
For Kids #3 ISBN: 978-1-944065-87-4
For Adults #1 ISBN: 978-1-944065-95-9
For Adults #2 ISBN: 978-1-944065-59-1
Challenger Edition #1 ISBN: 978-1-944065-65-2
Challenger Edition #2 ISBN: 978-1-944065-98-0

<u>Geometrics & Kaleidoscopes</u>

For Kids #1 ISBN: 978-1-944065-28-7
For Kids #2 ISBN: 978-1-944065-63-8
For Kids #3 ISBN: 978-1-944065-86-7
For Adults #1 ISBN: 978-1-944065-88-1
For Adults #2 ISBN: 978-1-944065-66-9
Challenger Edition #1 ISBN: 978-1-944065-58-4
Challenger Edition #2 ISBN: 978-1-944065-29-4

<u>Kaleidoscopes & Mandalas</u>

For Kids #1 ISBN: 978-1-944065-64-5
For Kids #2 ISBN: 978-1-944065-30-0
For Kids #3 ISBN: 978-1-944065-82-9
For Adults #1 ISBN: 978-1-944065-73-7
For Adults #2 ISBN: 978-1-944065-84-3
Challenger Edition #1 ISBN: 978-1-944065-46-1
Challenger Edition #2 ISBN: 978-1-944065-94-2

<u>Spheres, Abstracts & Mandalas</u>

Book One ISBN: 978-1-944065-97-3
Book Two ISBN: 978-1-944065-31-7

<u>Spheres, Abstracts & Geometrics</u>

Book One ISBN: 978-1-944065-77-5
Book Two ISBN: 978-1-944065-96-6

Spheres, Abstracts & Kaleidoscopes

Book One ISBN: 978-1-944065-34-8
Book Two ISBN: 978-1-944065-45-4

LittleSquareColoringBook.com

www.ingramcontent.com/pod-product-compliance
Lightning Source LLC
LaVergne TN
LVHW010108110826
845155LV00028B/538
9781944065089